MW00896883

# VIETNAMESE
## COOKBOOK

*70 Easy Recipes for Asian Foods from Vietnam.*

**Maki Blanc**

© **Copyright 2021 by Maki Blanc - All rights reserved.**

This document is geared towards providing exact and reliable information in regard to the topic and issue covered. The publication is sold with the idea that the publisher is not required to render accounting, officially permitted, or otherwise, qualified services. If advice is necessary, legal or professional, a practiced individual in the profession should be ordered.

From a Declaration of Principles which was accepted and approved equally by a Committee of the American Bar Association and a Committee of Publishers and Associations.

In no way is it legal to reproduce, duplicate, or transmit any part of this document in either electronic means or in printed format. Recording of this publication is strictly prohibited and any storage of this document is not allowed unless with written permission from the publisher. All rights reserved.

The information provided herein is stated to be truthful and consistent, in that any liability, in terms of inattention or otherwise, by any usage or abuse of any policies, processes, or directions contained within is the solitary and utter responsibility of the recipient reader. Under no circumstances will any legal responsibility or blame be held against the publisher for any reparation, damages, or monetary loss due to the information herein, either directly or indirectly.

Respective authors own all copyrights not held by the publisher.

The information herein is offered for informational purposes solely and is universal as so. The presentation of the information is without contract or any type of guarantee assurance.

The trademarks that are used are without any consent, and the publication of the trademark is without permission or backing by the trademark owner. All trademarks and brands within this book are for clarifying purposes only and are owned by the owners themselves, not affiliated with this document.

# Contents

# Introduction

Although culinary art of Asian countries has long been globally admired for numerous delicious and elaborately-ornamented dishes, Vietnamese cuisine still wins the heart of numerous foodies nationally and internationally due to its fresh ingredients, refreshing taste and exquisite presentation.

Culinary culture is normally shaped by the way a society lives. The Vietnamese culture promotes the addition of various new flavors into their food. No explorers have yet succeeded in resisting the amazing flavors of Vietnamese dishes.

The food of the north is intensely inspired by China with its sautés and noodle-based soups. As you move to the south, there are more flavors of Thailand and Cambodia in the Vietnamese food. The heat and humidity in the south region of Vietnam is favorable for rice paddies, coconut forests, jackfruit trees, and spice gardens. The food in southern Vietnam is usually more flavorful i.e. better flavors for pho, more palm sugar utilized in exquisite dishes, and those well-known taffy-like coconut confectioners made with the help of coconut cream.

In this book, you will learn various different recipes originated from Vietnam. The recipe section will include breakfast, lunch, dinner, snacks, and sweet dishes. All these recipes are detailed with easy to follow instructions and detailed ingredients that help you out in cooking by these at home. So, start reading this amazing book now.

# Chapter 1: The World of Vietnamese Breakfast Recipes

The morning meal in Vietnam is viewed as the main feast of the day. In various societies, they start the day with their own novel dishes. Following are the recipes listed below:

## 1.1 Vietnamese Fried Egg Recipe

**Preparation Time:** 30 minutes
**Cooking Time:** 10 minutes
**Serving:** 4

### Ingredients:

- Spring onions, four
- Rice noodles, two cups
- Pepper to taste
- Butter, as required
- Salt to taste
- Baby plum tomatoes, four
- Eggs, four
- Cilantro, half cup

### Instructions:
1. Boil the rice noodles according to the instructions on the package.
2. Once cooked, drain the noodles.
3. Put the butter in a pan.
4. Add the spring onions and chili into the small pan.
5. Cook for a couple of minutes until softened.

6. Whisk the milk and eggs in a bowl.
7. Add the eggs to the pan.
8. Fry the eggs.
9. Add the tomatoes and coriander leaves on top.
10. Once cooked, dish it out.
11. Add the eggs on top of the noodles.
12. The dish is ready to be served.

## 1.2 Vietnamese Breakfast Burgers Recipe

**Preparation Time:** 20 minutes
**Cooking Time:** 20 minutes
**Serving:** 4

**Ingredients:**

- Jalapenos, as required
- Chicken filet, four
- Mayonnaise, half cup
- Carrots, two
- Butter, two tablespoon
- Eggs, eight
- Burger buns, four
- Fish sauce, as required
- Cucumber, two
- Salt and pepper, to taste
- Cooking oil, as required

**Instructions:**
1. Take a large bowl.
2. Add the dry ingredients in a bowl.
3. Mix all the ingredients well.
4. Cook the chicken filet in a pan full of oil.

5. Dish out the chicken when it turns golden brown from both sides.
6. Toast the buns by adding a little butter on both sides.
7. Assemble the burgers.
8. Add all the ingredients one by one on top of the bun.
9. You can serve the burgers with any preferred sauce.
10.    The dish is ready to be served.

## 1.3 Vietnamese Steamed Rice Rolls with Pork Recipe

**Preparation Time:** 30 minutes
**Cooking Time:** 15 minutes
**Serving:** 4

### Ingredients:

- Thin soy sauce, one tablespoon
- Pepper powder, half tablespoon
- Sugar, one tablespoon
- Garlic powder, one tablespoon
- Fresh shallot, half tablespoon
- Milk, one cup
- Vegetable oil, one tablespoon
- Steamed rice, one cup
- Whole wheat flour, half cup
- Salt, to taste
- Water, to knead
- Pulled pork, one cup
- Yeast, two teaspoon

**Instructions:**

1. Take a bowl and add the steamed rice into it.
2. Then add the yeast and sugar into it.
3. Add lukewarm water in it.
4. Set aside for half hour.
5. Add the whole wheat flour into it.
6. Then add the salt and some water in it.
7. Then combine the ingredients to form a soft dough.
8. Meanwhile, mix the pulled pork and rest of the filling ingredients
9. Make round forms of dough with the help of the oil.
10. Add the mixture in middle of the dough and place on a tray.
11. Seam the rolls for fifteen minutes.
12. Your dish is ready to be served.

## 1.4 Vietnamese Crepes Recipe

**Preparation Time:** 10 minutes
**Cooking Time:** 15 minutes
**Serving:** 2

### Ingredients:

- Almond milk, one cup
- Cilantro as required
- Almond oil, two tablespoon
- Tapioca flour, half cup
- Almond flour, half cup
- Eggs, three
- Arrowroot starch, half teaspoon

**Instructions:**

1. Mix in both the flours in a bowl.
2. Mix the ingredients carefully.
3. Add the mixture in small quantities in a pan.
4. Let the crepes turn golden on both sides.
5. Add a little cilantro on top of your crepes.
6. You can add fresh fruits as well on the top.
7. You can garnish the crepes with any other ingredient that you prefer.
8. Your dish is ready to be served.

## 1.5 Vietnamese Breakfast Bowl Recipe

**Preparation Time:** 10 minutes
**Cooking Time:** 20 minutes
**Serving:** 4

### Ingredients:

- Coconut milk, half cup
- Wild blueberries, one cup
- Coconut oil, one tablespoon
- Sliced almonds, two tablespoon
- Milk, two cups
- Almond extract, one teaspoon
- Dry rolled oats, one cup
- Coconut cream, one cup

### Instructions:
1. Combine all the ingredients together in a bowl.
2. Pour the mixture into a baking dish coated with coconut oil.
3. Add the one cup of frozen wild blueberries on top.
4. Sprinkle the sliced almonds on top.
5. Set the dishes on a flat sheet pan.

6. Bake for twenty-five minutes in a preheated oven.
7. When cooked, dish out and add fresh berries on top.
8. Your dish is ready to be served.

## 1.6 Vietnamese Happy Pancakes Recipe

**Preparation Time:** 20 minutes
**Cooking Time:** 20 minutes
**Serving:** 4

### Ingredients:

- Sliced apples, one cup
- Sugar, four tablespoon
- Salt, as required
- Cilantro as required
- Sesame oil, two tablespoon
- Tapioca flour, half cup
- Almond flour, half cup
- Sliced peaches, one cup
- Coconut cream, a quarter cup
- Coconut milk, one cup

**Instructions:**
1. Mix in both the flours in a bowl.
2. Add the sliced peaches and apples into the bowl.
3. Add in the sugar and rest of the ingredients.
4. Mix the ingredients carefully.
5. Grease a pan with sesame oil.
6. Add the mixture in small quantities in a pan.
7. Let the pancakes turn golden on both sides.
8. Add a little cilantro on top of the pancakes.

9. You can garnish the pancakes with any other topping that you prefer.
10.        Your dish is ready to be served.

## 1.7 Vietnamese Breakfast Pastries Recipe

**Preparation Time:** 2 hours
**Cooking Time:** 10 minutes
**Serving:** 4

### Ingredients:

- Salt, to taste
- Pepper, to taste
- Milk, two cups
- White sugar, half cup
- Salt, one teaspoon
- Eggs, two
- Cooked ground pork, one cup
- Fish sauce, one teaspoon
- Oyster sauce, one teaspoon
- All-purpose flour, two cups
- Butter, one cup
- Dry yeast, one cup

### Instructions:
1. Take a medium bowl and add the butter in it.
2. Add the flour and mix well.
3. Then refrigerate it.
4. Take a large bowl and add the yeast into it.

5. Add the sugar, salt and milk.
6. Mix the warm milk mixture with the flour and the yeast.
7. Add the eggs, the lemon extract and the almond extract together.
8. Then knead it in the flour until the dough is formed.
9. Place butter on dough and fold it.
10.      Make pastries from the dough roll.
11.      Take a small bowl.
12.      Add the pork, salt, pepper and the sauces.
13.      Add the pork mixture in the pastry dough.
14.      Bake them for ten minutes.
15.      The pastry is ready to be served.

## 1.8 Vietnamese Scrambled Eggs with Fish Sauce Recipe

**Preparation Time:** 30 minutes
**Cooking Time:** 10 minutes
**Serving:** 4

**Ingredients:**

- Onions, one
- Chopped garlic, one teaspoon
- Butter, two tablespoon
- Fish sauce, half cup
- Mixed vegetables, half pound
- Salt, to taste
- Black pepper, to taste
- Chopped fresh chives, as required
- Eggs, twelve

**Instructions:**

1. Take a large pan.
2. Add the butter and let it meltdown.
3. Add in the chopped onion.
4. Cook the onion until soft.
5. Add in the garlic.
6. Mix the onions and garlic for two minutes and add in the mixed vegetables.
7. Add the eggs and let them cook.
8. Scramble the mixture.
9. Add in the salt and pepper.
10. Add in the fish sauce in the end.
11. When the eggs are done, dish them out.
12. Add the fresh chopped chives on top.
13. Your dish is ready to be served.

## 1.9 Vietnamese Steak and Eggs Recipe

**Preparation Time:** 10 minutes
**Cooking Time:** 20 minutes
**Serving:** 4

**Ingredients:**

- Powdered garlic, half teaspoon
- Eggs, four
- Steak meat, half pound
- Turmeric, half teaspoon
- Mixed vegetables, one cup
- Sea salt, to taste
- Coconut oil, two tablespoon
- Mixed spice, half teaspoon
- Onion, one
- Fish sauce, one tablespoon

- Oyster sauce, two tablespoon
- Dried thyme, half teaspoon
- Powdered ginger, half teaspoon

## Instructions:
1. Heat the coconut oil in a pan.
2. Add the steak meat.
3. Dish out the meat when done and slice it up.
4. Add the mixed vegetables and spices.
5. Once they turn soft, add in the eggs as well.
6. Add the spices and cook it for five to ten minutes or until the eggs are cooked.
7. Add in the sliced steaks.
8. Mix the dish well and cook for five minutes.
9. Your dish is ready to be served.

# 1.10 Vietnamese Scrambled Eggs with Pork Mince Recipe

**Preparation Time:** 30 minutes
**Cooking Time:** 10 minutes
**Serving:** 4

### Ingredients:

- Onions, one
- Chopped garlic, one teaspoon

- Butter, two tablespoon
- Fish sauce, half cup
- Oyster sauce, half tablespoon
- Mixed spices, one tablespoon
- Pork mince, half pound
- Salt, to taste
- Black pepper, to taste
- Chopped fresh chives, as required
- Eggs, twelve

**Instructions:**
1. Take a large pan.
2. Add the butter and let it meltdown.
3. Add in the chopped onion.
4. Cook the onion until soft.
5. Add in the garlic.
6. Mix the onions and garlic for two minutes and add in the minced pork.
7. Add the eggs and let it cook.
8. Scramble the mixture.
9. Add in the salt, mixed spice and pepper.
10. Add in the fish sauce and the oyster sauce in the end.
11. When the eggs are done dish them out.
12. Add the fresh chopped chives on top.
13. Your dish is ready to be served.

## 1.11 Vietnamese Breakfast Egg Rolls Recipe

**Preparation Time:** 15 minutes
**Cooking Time:** 25 minutes
**Serving:** 4

**Ingredients:**

- Cooked eggs, three
- Canola oil, one cup
- Minced garlic, two tablespoon
- Chopped red onion, one cup
- Coconut milk, one cup
- Lime juice, two tablespoon
- Water, as required
- Wonton wrappers, as required
- Cilantro leaves, as required
- Salt, a pinch

**Instructions:**
1. Take a bowl.
2. Add the eggs and garlic powder.
3. Add more oil into it and add all the ingredients.
4. Add the chopped red onions, coconut milk and water as required.
5. Add the lime juice and cilantro leaves into it.
6. Add the salt and pepper as required.
7. Add the ingredients into the wrappers and roll them.
8. Serve the rolls with soy sauce.
9. Your dish is ready to be served.

# 1.12 Vietnamese Tofu Pancakes Recipe

**Preparation Time:** 20 minutes
**Cooking Time:** 20 minutes
**Serving:** 4

**Ingredients:**

- Ground garlic, half teaspoon
- Salt, as required
- Black pepper, two
- Ground pepper, as required
- Red onion, one
- Cilantro as required
- Sesame oil, two tablespoon
- Tapioca flour, half cup
- Almond flour, half cup
- Shredded tofu, one cup
- Coconut milk, one cup
- Fish sauce, half teaspoon
- Ground ginger, half teaspoon

**Instructions:**
1. Mix in both the flours in a bowl.
2. Add the chopped red onions.
3. Add the shredded tofu into the bowl.
4. Add in the spices, black pepper, fish sauce and cilantro.
5. Mix the ingredients carefully.
6. Grease a pan with sesame oil.
7. Add the mixture in small quantities in a pan.
8. Let the pancakes turn golden on both sides.
9. Add a little cilantro on top of your pancakes.
10. Your dish is ready to be served.

# Chapter 2: The World of Vietnamese Lunch Recipes

Large numbers of the most famous Vietnamese dishes can be made very easily at home. Following are some classic Vietnamese recipes that are rich in healthy nutrients and you can easily make them with the detailed instructions list in each recipe:

## 2.1 Vietnamese Prawn and Papaya Salad Recipe

**Preparation Time:** 10 minutes
**Cooking Time:** 30 minutes
**Serving:** 2

### Ingredients:

- Prawn pieces, half pound
- Maple syrup, one teaspoon
- Ground ginger, a quarter teaspoon
- Papaya, two
- Mixed nuts, two tablespoon
- Pepper, as required
- Cilantro, half cup
- Salt, a quarter teaspoon
- Soy sauce, as required
- Mint leaves, half cup
- Salad dressing, half cup

**Instructions:**
1. Peel the papaya and then cut into large pieces.

2. Boil the prawn pieces, drain them and slice them into a bowl.
3. Mix all the ingredients along with the prawns and papaya.
4. In a bowl, add the salad dressing and beat it well.
5. Drizzle the dressing on top of the prawns and papaya mixture.
6. Your dish is ready to be served.

## 2.2 Vietnamese Chicken Salad Recipes

**Preparation Time:** 10 minutes
**Cooking Time:** 30 minutes
**Serving:** 2

### Ingredients:

- Chicken pieces, half pound
- Maple syrup, one teaspoon
- Ground ginger, a quarter teaspoon
- Mixed fruit, half cup
- Mixed nuts, two tablespoon
- Pepper, as required
- Cilantro, half cup
- Salt, a quarter teaspoon
- Soy sauce, as required
- Mint leaves, half cup
- Salad dressing, half cup

**Instructions:**

1. Peel the fruits and then cut them into large pieces.
2. Boil the chicken pieces, drain them and slice them into a bowl.
3. Mix all the ingredients along with the chicken and fruits.
4. In a bowl, add the salad dressing and beat it well.
5. Drizzle the dressing on top of the chicken and fruit mixture.
6. Your dish is ready to be served.

## 2.3 Vietnamese Herb Salad Recipe

**Preparation Time:** 10 minutes
**Cooking Time:** 30 minutes
**Serving:** 2

**Ingredients:**

- Parsley leaves, half pound
- Maple syrup, one teaspoon
- Sliced celery, a quarter teaspoon
- Fresh dill leaves, half cup
- Roasted cashews, half cup
- Pepper, as required
- Cilantro, half cup
- Salt, a quarter teaspoon
- Soy sauce, as required
- Basil leaves, half cup
- Fresh fruit as required
- Salad dressing, half cup

**Instructions:**
1. Peel the leaves and then cut them into large pieces.
2. Mix all the ingredients along with the leaves and fruits.
3. In a bowl, add the salad dressing and beat it well.
4. Drizzle the dressing on top of the leaves and fruit mixture.
5. Your dish is ready to be served.

## 2.4 Vietnamese Summer Rolls with Peanut Dipping Sauce Recipe

**Preparation Time:** 10 minutes
**Cooking Time:** 20 minutes
**Serving:** 2

**Ingredients:**

- Olive oil, two cups
- Garlic powder, one tablespoon
- Salt to taste
- Pepper to taste
- Paprika, one tablespoon
- Onion diced, one cup
- Parsley, one tablespoon
- Pork meat, one cup
- Tomatoes, one cup
- Jalapeno slices, as required
- Peanut dipping sauce, one cup
- Avocado slices, as required
- Tortilla sheets, four

**Instructions:**

1. Add the olive oil into a pan.
2. Heat the oil well.
3. Add the onions.
4. Cook the onions well until they turn soft.
5. Add parsley, garlic powder, paprika and tomatoes.
6. Cook them for five minutes.
7. Cook the mixture again and keep stirring.
8. Add pieces of pork meat.
9. Continue to cook the ingredients for few minutes.
10. Lay the mixture onto a tortilla sheet.
11. Add the peanut dipping sauce on top of the meat.
12. Add the rest of the ingredients on top and roll it into a roll.
13. Heat the roll.
14. You can serve it with any other sauce of your choice.
15. Your dish is ready to be served.

## 2.5 Vietnamese Pork Meatballs Recipe

**Preparation Time:** 30 minutes
**Cooking Time:** 10 minutes
**Serving:** 4

**Ingredients:**

- Soy sauce, two tablespoon
- Eggs, two
- Salt, to taste
- Black pepper, to taste
- Milk, one cup
- Onion, one cup

- Bread crumbs, one cup
- Sugar, two tablespoon
- Minced pork meat, one pound
- Minced ginger, two tablespoon
- Cayenne pepper, a dash
- Butter, two tablespoon
- All-purpose flour, five tablespoon

**Instructions:**

1. Take a large bowl.
2. Add the oil and onions into the bowl.
3. Add the chopped ginger into the bowl.
4. Add the minced pork into the bowl.
5. Add the spices, eggs and bread crumbs.
6. Mix all the ingredients together.
7. Shape the pork mixture into round meatballs.
8. Heat a grilling pan.
9. Add the olive oil on top.
10. Place the meatballs on top.
11. Fry the meatballs on both sides until it turns golden brown.
12. Fry all the meatballs and dish them out.
13. The dish is ready to be served.

# 2.6 Vietnamese Chicken Pho Recipe

**Preparation Time:** 30 minutes
**Cooking Time:** 20 minutes
**Serving:** 4

**Ingredients:**

- Shredded chicken, one cup
- Onion, one cup

- Rice noodles, one cup
- Chinese paprika, half teaspoon
- Water, one cup
- Minced garlic, two tablespoon
- Minced ginger, two tablespoon
- Cilantro, half cup
- Olive oil, two tablespoon
- Water, half cup
- Chicken stock, half cup
- Chopped tomatoes, one cup

**Instructions:**
1. Take a pan.
2. Add in the oil and onions.
3. Cook the onions until they become soft and fragrant.
4. Add in the chopped garlic and ginger.
5. Cook the mixture and add the tomatoes into it.
6. Add the spices.
7. When the tomatoes are done, add the shredded chicken and stock into it.
8. Mix the ingredients carefully and cover your pan.
9. Add the rice noodles into the mixture.
10. Add the water into the mixture and cover the pan.
11. Let the pho cook for ten to fifteen minutes straight.
12. Add cilantro on top.
13. Your dish is ready to be served.

## 2.7 Vietnamese Baked Snapper Recipe

**Preparation Time:** 10 minutes

**Cooking Time:** 25 minutes
**Serving:** 2

### Ingredients:

- Powdered cumin, one tablespoon
- Salt, to taste
- Black pepper, to taste
- Turmeric powder, one teaspoon
- Onion, one cup
- Smoked paprika, half teaspoon
- Hoison sauce, half cup
- Snapper pieces, one pound
- Minced garlic, two tablespoon
- Minced ginger, two tablespoon
- Cilantro, half cup
- Olive oil, two tablespoon
- Oyster sauce, three tablespoon
- Roasted peanuts, half cup

## Instructions:
1. Take a large bowl.
2. Add the oil and onions into the bowl.
3. Add the chopped garlic and ginger into the bowl.
4. Add the tomatoes into the bowl.
5. Add the spices.
6. Add the cilantro into it.
7. Mix all the ingredients together.
8. Cover your snapper pieces with the mixture above.
9. Bake your snapper pieces.
10. Dish them out when cooked properly.
11. Sprinkle some cilantro and roasted peanuts on top.

12.    You can serve it with any of your preferred sauces.

13.    Your dish is ready to be served.

## 2.8 Vietnamese Stir-Fried Sweet Shrimp Recipe

**Preparation Time:** 30 minutes
**Cooking Time:** 10 minutes
**Serving:** 4

### Ingredients:

- Fish broth, one cup
- Honey, one teaspoon
- Onion, one cup
- Brown sugar, two tablespoon
- Smoked paprika, half teaspoon
- Water, one cup
- Shrimps, two cups
- Mixed spices, two tablespoon
- Minced garlic, two tablespoon
- Minced ginger, two tablespoon
- Cilantro, half cup
- Olive oil, two tablespoon
- Chopped tomatoes, one cup

### Instructions:
1. Take a pan.
2. Add in the oil and onions.
3. Cook the onions until they become soft and fragrant.
4. Add in the chopped garlic and ginger.
5. Cook the mixture and add the tomatoes into it.

6. Add the spices, honey, sugar and sauces.
7. When the tomatoes are done, add the shrimps into it.
8. Cook for five minutes.
9. When cooked, dish it out.
10.    Garnish your dish with chopped cilantro leaves
11.    Your dish is ready to be served.

## 2.9 Vietnamese Lemongrass and Tamarind Chicken Recipe

**Preparation Time:** 30 minutes
**Cooking Time:** 10 minutes
**Serving:** 4

### Ingredients:

- Cilantro, half cup
- Sesame oil, two tablespoon
- Chopped tomatoes, one cup
- Lemon juice, one cup
- Powdered cumin, one tablespoon
- Salt, to taste
- Black pepper, to taste
- Lemongrass, one teaspoon
- Onion, one cup
- Vegetable broth, one cup
- Chinese paprika, half teaspoon
- Chicken cubes, two cup
- Tamarind paste, half cup
- Minced garlic, two tablespoon
- Minced ginger, two tablespoon

**Instructions:**

1. Take a pan.
2. Add in the oil and onions.
3. Cook the onions until they become soft and fragrant.
4. Add in the chopped garlic and ginger.
5. Cook the mixture and add the tomatoes into it.
6. Add the spices.
7. When the tomatoes are done, add the chicken cubes into it.
8. Cook for five minutes.
9. Add in the lemongrass and tamarind paste.
10. Add in the broth and lemon juice.
11. Mix the ingredients carefully and cover the pan.
12. When cooked, dish it out.
13. Garnish the dish with chopped cilantro leaves
14. Your dish is ready to be served.

## 2.10 Vietnamese Marinated Lamb Chops Recipe

**Preparation Time:** 10 minutes
**Cooking Time:** 25 minutes
**Serving:** 2

**Ingredients:**

- Lemon juice, one tablespoon
- Salt, to taste

- Black pepper, to taste
- Mix spice, one teaspoon
- Onion, one cup
- Smoked paprika, half teaspoon
- Lamb chops, one pound
- Minced garlic, two tablespoon
- Minced ginger, two tablespoon
- Cilantro, half cup
- Olive oil, two tablespoon

**Instructions:**
1. Take a large bowl.
2. Add the oil and onions into the bowl.
3. Add the chopped garlic and ginger into the bowl.
4. Add the spices.
5. Add the cilantro into it.
6. Mix all the ingredients together.
7. Add the lamb chops into the mixture.
8. Cook the lamb chops.
9. Dish them out when cooked properly.
10. Sprinkle some cilantro on top.
11. Your dish is ready to be served.

# 2.11 Vietnamese Cabbage Soup Recipe

**Preparation Time:** 30 minutes
**Cooking Time:** 20 minutes
**Serving:** 4

## Ingredients:

- Sliced cabbage, one cup
- Eggs, two
- Onion, one cup

- Chinese paprika, half teaspoon
- Water, one cup
- Minced garlic, two tablespoon
- Minced ginger, two tablespoon
- Cilantro, half cup
- Olive oil, two tablespoon
- Water, half cup
- Vegetable stock, half cup
- Chopped tomatoes, one cup

**Instructions:**
1. Take a pan.
2. Add in the oil and onions.
3. Cook the onions until they become soft and fragrant.
4. Add in the chopped garlic and ginger.
5. Cook the mixture and add the tomatoes into it.
6. Add the spices.
7. When the tomatoes are done, add the sliced cabbage and stock into it.
8. Mix the ingredients carefully and cover your pan.
9. Let the soup cook for ten to fifteen minutes straight.
10. Add cilantro on top.
11. Your dish is ready to be served.

## 2.12 Vietnamese Mixed Vegetables Recipe

**Preparation Time:** 30 minutes
**Cooking Time:** 10 minutes
**Serving:** 4

**Ingredients:**

- Chopped tomatoes, one cup
- Cauliflower, one cup
- Mix spice powder, one teaspoon
- Onion, one cup
- Fish sauce, a quarter cup
- Oyster sauce, a quarter cup
- Brussel sprouts, one cup
- Smoked paprika, half teaspoon
- Chopped carrots, one cup
- Minced garlic, two tablespoon
- Minced ginger, two tablespoon
- Lemon juice, half cup
- Chopped bell peppers, one cup
- Olive oil, two tablespoon

**Instructions:**
1. Take a pan.
2. Add in the oil and onions.
3. Cook the onions until they become soft and fragrant.
4. Add in the chopped garlic and ginger.
5. Cook the mixture and add the tomatoes to it.
6. Add the spices.
7. When the tomatoes are done, add the vegetables into it.
8. Mix the ingredients carefully and cover the pan.
9. When your vegetables are done, dish them out.
10.     Add cilantro on top.
11.     Your dish is ready to be served.

## 2.13 Vietnamese Fried Rice Recipe

**Preparation Time:** 10 minutes
**Cooking Time:** 25 minutes
**Serving:** 2

## Ingredients:

- Minced garlic, two tablespoon
- Minced ginger, two tablespoon
- Cilantro, half cup
- Cooked rice, one cup
- Olive oil, two tablespoon
- Coconut cream, three tablespoon
- Chopped tomatoes, one cup
- Water, one cup
- Fish sauce, one teaspoon
- Onion, one cup
- Coconut milk, one cup
- Smoked paprika, half teaspoon
- Water, one cup

## Instructions:
1. Take a pan.
2. Add in the oil and onions.
3. Cook the onions until they become soft and fragrant.
4. Add in the chopped garlic and ginger.
5. Cook the mixture and add the tomatoes into it.
6. Add the spices.
7. When the tomatoes are done, add the coconut milk into it.
8. Add in the water.
9. Mix the ingredients carefully and cover your pan.
10. Add in the rice and into the mixture.

11.      Fry the rice and let it cook for an additional five minutes.
12.      Add cilantro on top.
13.      Your dish is ready to be served.

## 2.14 Vietnamese Pork Chops Recipe

**Preparation Time:** 10 minutes
**Cooking Time:** 20 minutes
**Serving:** 2

### Ingredients:

- Fish sauce, half teaspoon
- Water, half cup
- Pork chops, one pound
- Minced garlic, two tablespoon
- Minced ginger, two tablespoon
- Cilantro, half cup
- Olive oil, two tablespoon
- Chopped tomatoes, one cup
- Lemon juice, one cup
- Oyster sauce, one tablespoon
- Salt, to taste
- Black pepper, to taste
- Mix spice, one teaspoon
- Onion, one cup
- pork broth, one cup

### Instructions:

1. Take a pan.
2. Add in the oil and onions.
3. Cook the onions until they become soft and fragrant.

4. Add in the chopped garlic and ginger.
5. Cook the mixture and add the tomatoes into it.
6. Add the spices.
7. When the tomatoes are done, add the pork chops into it.
8. Add in the water and lemon juice.
9. Mix the ingredients carefully and cover the pan.
10.      Garnish the dish with chopped cilantro.
11.      Your dish is ready to be served.

## 2.15 Vietnamese Instant Pho Soup Recipe

**Preparation Time:** 30 minutes
**Cooking Time:** 20 minutes
**Serving:** 4

**Ingredients:**

- Pork, two cup
- Onion, one cup
- Rice noodles, one cup
- Oyster sauce, half teaspoon
- Water, one cup
- Minced garlic, two tablespoon
- Minced ginger, two tablespoon
- Cilantro, half cup
- Fish sauce, two tablespoon
- Olive oil, two tablespoon
- Chicken stock, half cup
- Chopped tomatoes, one cup

**Instructions:**
1. Take an instant pot.
2. Add in the oil and onions.

3. Cook the onions until they become soft and fragrant.
4. Add in the chopped garlic and ginger.
5. Cook the mixture and add the tomatoes into it.
6. Add the spices.
7. When the tomatoes are done, add the minced pork and stock into it.
8. Mix the ingredients carefully and cover your pot.
9. Let the pho cook for ten to fifteen minutes straight.
10. Add the rice noodles into the pot and cook for five minutes.
11. Add cilantro on top.
12. Your dish is ready to be served.

# Chapter 3: The World of Vietnamese Dinner Recipes

Vegetables and noodles are the standard eating routine in many families in the cities of Vietnam. A typical Vietnamese feast will usually incorporate rice, a meat or fish dish, soups and vegetables. Following are some classic dinner recipes that are rich in healthy nutrients and you can easily make them with the detailed instructions list in each recipe:

## 3.1 Vietnamese Sambal Kangkung with Shrimp Paste Recipe

**Preparation Time:** 30 minutes
**Cooking Time:** 10 minutes
**Serving:** 4

### Ingredients:

- Sambal olek, one tablespoon
- Cilantro, half cup
- Sesame oil, two tablespoon
- Chopped tomatoes, one cup
- shrimp paste, one cup
- Powdered cumin, one tablespoon
- Salt, to taste
- Black pepper, to taste
- Lemongrass, one teaspoon
- Chinese paprika, half teaspoon
- Diced kangkung, one pound
- Tamarind paste, half cup
- Minced garlic, two tablespoon
- Minced ginger, two tablespoon

**Instructions:**
1. Take a pan.
2. Add in the oil and onions.
3. Cook the onions until they become soft and fragrant.
4. Add in the chopped garlic and ginger.
5. Cook the mixture and add the tomatoes into it.
6. Add the spices.
7. When the tomatoes are done, add the kangkung and shrimp paste into it.
8. Cook for five minutes.
9. Add in the sambal olek, lemongrass and tamarind paste.
10. Mix the ingredients carefully and cover the pan.
11. When cooked, dish it out.
12. Garnish the dish with chopped cilantro leaves
13. Your dish is ready to be served.

# 3.2 Vietnamese Pomelo and Shrimp Salad Recipe

**Preparation Time:** 10 minutes
**Cooking Time:** 30 minutes
**Serving:** 2

**Ingredients:**

- Cooked shrimps, half pound
- Bean sprouts, one cup
- Sliced celery, a quarter teaspoon
- Fresh basil leaves, half cup

- Pomelo pulp, half cup
- Pepper, as required
- Cilantro, half cup
- Salt, a quarter teaspoon
- Soy sauce, as required
- Bird's eye chili, half cup
- Salad dressing, half cup

**Instructions:**
1. Cut the bean sprouts into large pieces.
2. Mix all the ingredients along with the shrimps.
3. In a bowl, add the salad dressing and beat it well.
4. Drizzle the dressing on top of the shrimps.
5. Your dish is ready to be served.

## 3.3 Vietnamese Pork Bone and Green Papaya Soup Recipe

**Preparation Time:** 10 minutes
**Cooking Time:** 10 minutes
**Serving:** 4

**Ingredients:**

- Chopped white onions, one cup
- Chopped green papaya, one pound
- Chicken stock, one quart
- Unsalted butter, three tablespoon
- Pork bones, half pound
- Fresh cilantro, as required
- Fresh herbs, half cup
- Dried thyme, one teaspoon
- Minced garlic, one teaspoon
- Fish sauce, half teaspoon

- Oyster sauce, two tablespoon

**Instructions:**
1. Take a large pan.
2. Add the chopped onions in the butter.
3. When soft and translucent, add in the minced garlic.
4. Add in the stock, and rest of the ingredients.
5. Add in all the rest of the ingredients and cook the ingredients until the papaya is cooked.
6. Remove the bone pieces.
7. Blend the soup well.
8. Cook the soup for an extra few minutes.
9. Add the soup in a serving bowl.
10. You can also garnish it with chopped fresh cilantro.
11. The dish is ready to be served.

# 3.4 Vietnamese Beef and Noodle Salad Recipe

**Preparation Time:** 10 minutes
**Cooking Time:** 25 minutes
**Serving:** 4

**Ingredients:**

- Cooked beef cubes, one cup
- Carrot sliced, one cup
- Red bell pepper sliced, one cup
- Ginger, one tablespoon
- Garlic powder, two teaspoon
- Fish sauce, half teaspoon
- Sesame oil, one teaspoon
- Soy sauce, one teaspoon

- Sriracha, one tablespoon
- Lime juice, one tablespoon
- Rice noodles, one pack
- Salt, to taste
- Pepper, to taste

## Instructions:

1. Take a large bowl and add beef cubes into it.
2. Add the ginger and garlic powder.
3. Mix well.
4. Add the carrot slices and red bell pepper into it.
5. Add the salt and pepper as you like.
6. Add the sesame oil and mix well so that a homogeneous mixture is obtained.
7. Add the sriracha and rest of the ingredients into the mixture.
8. Mix all the ingredients.
9. Your salad is ready to be served.

## 3.5 Vietnamese Lamb Shanks with Sweet Potatoes Recipe

**Preparation Time:** 30 minutes
**Cooking Time:** 10 minutes
**Serving:** 4

### Ingredients:

- Cooked sweet potatoes, two cup
- Mix spice, one teaspoon
- Onion, one cup
- Smoked paprika, half teaspoon
- Chinese dried chilies, half cup
- Minced garlic, two tablespoon
- Minced ginger, two tablespoon

- Lemon juice, half cup
- Oyster sauce, half cup
- Lamb shanks, half pound
- Olive oil, two tablespoon
- Chopped tomatoes, one cup

**Instructions:**
1. Take a pan.
2. Add in the oil and onions.
3. Cook the onions until they become soft and fragrant.
4. Add in the chopped garlic and ginger.
5. Cook the mixture and add the tomatoes into it.
6. Add the spices.
7. When the tomatoes are done, add the sweet potato and rest of the ingredients into it.
8. Mix the ingredients carefully.
9. Add cilantro on top.
10. Your dish is ready to be served.

# 3.6 Vietnamese Spiced Duck Salad Recipe

**Preparation Time:** 10 minutes
**Cooking Time:** 10 minutes
**Serving:** 2

### Ingredients:

- Roasted duck, half pound
- Spicy red sauce, one cup
- Sliced celery, a quarter teaspoon
- Fresh basil leaves, half cup
- Sirarcha, half cup
- Pepper, as required
- Cilantro, half cup
- Salt, a quarter teaspoon
- Soy sauce, as required
- Bird's eye chili, half cup
- Salad dressing, half cup

### Instructions:
1. Cut the duck meat into large pieces.
2. Mix all the ingredients along with the duck meat.
3. In a bowl, add the salad dressing and beat it well.
4. Drizzle the dressing on top of the meat.
5. Your dish is ready to be served.

# 3.7 Vietnamese Seafood Salad Recipe

**Preparation Time:** 10 minutes
**Cooking Time:** 10 minutes
**Serving:** 2

### Ingredients:

- Mixed seafood, half pound
- Wine vinegar, one cup
- Caster sugar, a quarter teaspoon
- Spring onions, half cup
- Bean sprouts, two cups
- Sirarcha, half cup
- Pepper, as required
- Cilantro, half cup
- Salt, a quarter teaspoon
- Soy sauce, as required
- Bird's eye chili, half cup
- Salad dressing, half cup

### Instructions:
1. Cook your seafood by boiling it well.
2. Mix all the ingredients along with the bean sprouts and spring onions.
3. In a bowl, add the salad dressing and beat it well.
4. Drizzle the dressing on top of the mixture.
5. Your dish is ready to be served.

# 3.8 Vietnamese Caramel Trout Recipe

**Preparation Time:** 30 minutes
**Cooking Time:** 10 minutes
**Serving:** 4

## Ingredients:

- Brown sugar, one tablespoon
- Cilantro, half cup
- Sesame oil, two tablespoon
- Chopped tomatoes, one cup
- Rainbow trout, one cup
- Oyster sauce, one tablespoon
- Salt, to taste
- Black pepper, to taste
- Lemongrass, one teaspoon
- Chinese paprika, half teaspoon
- Steamed rice, one cup
- Minced garlic, two tablespoon
- Minced ginger, two tablespoon

## Instructions:
1. Take a pan.
2. Add in the oil and onions.
3. Cook the onions until they become soft and fragrant.
4. Add in the chopped garlic and ginger.
5. Cook the mixture and add the tomatoes into it.
6. Add the spices.
7. When the tomatoes are done, add the trout into it.
8. Cook for five minutes.
9. Add in the brown sugar, lemongrass and steamed rice.
10. Mix the ingredients carefully and cover the pan.
11. When cooked, dish it out.

12.     Garnish the dish with chopped cilantro leaves.
13.     Your dish is ready to be served.

---

## 3.9 Vietnamese Veggie Hotpot Recipe

**Preparation Time:** 20 minutes
**Cooking Time:** 20 minutes
**Serving:** 4

### Ingredients:

- Oyster sauce, one tablespoon
- Chinese chili peppers, two
- Fish sauce, one tablespoon
- Soy sauce, half tablespoon
- Minced garlic, two teaspoon
- Cooking oil, three tablespoon
- Hot sauce, half cup
- Mixed vegetables, two cups
- Salt, as required
- Chopped fresh cilantro, as required

### Instructions:
1. Take a large pan.
2. Add the cooking oil into the pan and heat it.
3. Add the vegetables into the pan and stir-fry it.
4. Add the minced garlic along with the vegetables.
5. Add the soy sauce, fish sauce, Chinese chili peppers, hot sauce and rest of the ingredients into the mixture.
6. Cook your dish for ten minutes.
7. Dish out your vegetables and garnish them with chopped fresh cilantro leaves.

8. Your dish is ready to be served.

## 3.10 Vietnamese Prawn and Noodle Salad with Crispy Shallots Recipe

**Preparation Time:** 10 minutes
**Cooking Time:** 25 minutes
**Serving:** 4

### Ingredients:

- Cooked prawns, one cup
- Carrot sliced, one cup
- Red bell pepper sliced, one cup
- Ginger, one tablespoon
- Garlic powder, two teaspoon
- Fish sauce, half teaspoon
- Sesame oil, one teaspoon
- Soy sauce, one teaspoon
- Sriracha, one tablespoon
- Lime juice, one tablespoon
- Rice noodles, one pack
- Salt, to taste
- Pepper, to taste
- Shallots, half cup

### Instructions:
1. Take a large bowl and add prawns into it.
2. Add the ginger and garlic powder.
3. Mix well.
4. Add the carrot slices and red bell pepper into it.
5. Add the salt and pepper as you like.
6. Add the sesame oil and mix well so that a homogeneous mixture is obtained.

7. Add the sriracha and rest of the ingredients into the mixture.
8. Fry the shallots in oil until they turn crispy.
9. Add the shallots on top of the mixture.
10.    Your salad is ready to be served.

## 3.11 Vietnamese Lemongrass Chicken Recipe

**Preparation Time:** 30 minutes
**Cooking Time:** 10 minutes
**Serving:** 4

**Ingredients:**

- Cilantro, half cup
- Sesame oil, two tablespoon
- Chopped tomatoes, one cup
- Lemon juice, one cup
- Fish sauce, one tablespoon
- Salt, to taste
- Black pepper, to taste
- Lemongrass, one teaspoon
- Onion, one cup
- Vegetable broth, one cup
- Chinese paprika, half teaspoon
- Chicken cubes, two cup
- Minced garlic, two tablespoon
- Minced ginger, two tablespoon

**Instructions:**
1. Take a pan.
2. Add in the oil and onions.
3. Cook the onions until they become soft and fragrant.

4. Add in the chopped garlic and ginger.
5. Cook the mixture and add the tomatoes into it.
6. Add the spices.
7. When the tomatoes are done, add the chicken cubes into it.
8. Cook for five minutes.
9. Add in the lemongrass.
10. Add in the broth and lemon juice.
11. Mix the ingredients carefully and cover the pan.
12. When cooked, dish it out.
13. Garnish the dish with chopped cilantro leaves
14. Your dish is ready to be served.

## 3.12 Vietnamese Garlic Butter Noodles Recipe

**Preparation Time:** 30 minutes
**Cooking Time:** 10 minutes
**Serving:** 4

### Ingredients:

- Butter, one tablespoon
- Cilantro, one cup
- Fresh ginger, one teaspoon
- Fish sauce, one tablespoon
- Soy sauce, one tablespoon
- Oyster sauce, half teaspoon
- Chili garlic sauce, two tablespoon
- Fresh cilantro leaves, half cup
- Fresh basil leaves, a quarter cup
- Vegetable broth, one cup

* Rice noodles, as required

**Instructions:**
1. Add all the ingredients of the sauce into a wok.
2. Cook your ingredients.
3. Add the noodles into the mixture once the sauce is ready.
4. Mix the noodles well and cook it for five minutes.
5. Add the cilantro into the dish.
6. Your dish is ready to be served.

# 3.13 Vietnamese Papaya Salad Recipe

**Preparation Time:** 10 minutes
**Cooking Time:** 30 minutes
**Serving:** 2

**Ingredients:**

* Maple syrup, one teaspoon
* Ground ginger, a quarter teaspoon
* Papaya, two
* Mixed nuts, two tablespoon
* Pepper, as required
* Cilantro, half cup
* Salt, a quarter teaspoon
* Soy sauce, as required
* Mint leaves, half cup
* Salad dressing, half cup

**Instructions:**

7. Peel the papaya and then cut into large pieces.
8. Mix all the ingredients along with the papaya.
9. In a bowl, add the salad dressing and beat it well.
10.     Drizzle the dressing on top of the papaya mixture.
11.     Your dish is ready to be served.

## 3.14 Vietnamese Purple Yam Soup Recipe

**Preparation Time:** 10 minutes
**Cooking Time:** 30 minutes
**Serving:** 4

### Ingredients:

- Chopped white onions, one cup
- Purple yam, one pound
- Fresh chopped cilantro, half cup
- Unsalted butter, three tablespoon
- Oyster sauce, one teaspoon
- Minced garlic, one teaspoon
- Fish sauce, half teaspoon
- Coconut milk, half cup
- Coconut cream, one cup

**Instructions:**
1. In a large pan, add the chopped onions in the butter.
2. Add in the minced garlic when onions are soft and translucent.
3. Add in the purple yam.
4. Add in all the rest of the ingredients and cook the ingredients until the purple yams are cooked.
5. Blend the soup well.

6. Cook for an extra few minutes.
7. The dish is ready to be served.

## 3.15 Vietnamese Fried Tofu Recipe

**Preparation Time:** 30 minutes
**Cooking Time:** 10 minutes
**Serving:** 4

### Ingredients:

- Cilantro, half cup
- Olive oil, two tablespoon
- Chopped tomatoes, one cup
- Lemon juice, half cup
- Mix spice powder, one tablespoon
- Salt, to taste
- Black pepper, to taste
- Fish sauce, one teaspoon
- Onion, one cup
- Tofu cubes, one cup
- Oyster sauce, half teaspoon
- Minced garlic, two tablespoon

### Instructions:
1. Take a pan.
2. Add in the oil and onions.
3. Cook the onions until they become soft and fragrant.
4. Add in the chopped garlic.
5. Cook the mixture and add the tomatoes into it.
6. Add the spices and sauces.
7. When the tomatoes are done, add the tofu cubes into it.
8. Cook for five minutes.

9. When cooked, dish it out.
10.     Garnish your dish with chopped cilantro leaves.
11.     Your dish is ready to be served.

## 3.16 Vietnamese Noodle Soup Recipe

**Preparation Time:** 10 minutes
**Cooking Time:** 20 minutes
**Serving:** 4

**Ingredients:**

- Minced garlic, two tablespoon
- Minced ginger, two tablespoon
- Cilantro, half cup
- Diced carrots, one cup
- Olive oil, two tablespoon
- Beef broth, half cup
- Fish sauce, half cup
- Vegetable stock, half cup
- Chopped tomatoes, one cup
- Chicken broth, one cup
- Hot sauce, half cup
- Onion, one cup
- Bell peppers, one cup
- Noodles, half pound
- Oyster sauce, half teaspoon
- Soy sauce, one cup

**Instructions:**
1. Take a pan.
2. Add in the oil and onions.

3. Cook the onions until they become soft and fragrant.
4. Add in the chopped garlic and ginger.
5. Cook the mixture and add the tomatoes into it.
6. Add the sauces.
7. When the tomatoes are done, add the noodles into it.
8. Add in both chicken and beef broth.
9. Mix the ingredients carefully and cover your pan.
10. Add the vegetables into the mixture.
11. Add the water into the mixture and cover the pan.
12. Let the soup cook for ten to fifteen minutes straight.
13. Add the cilantro on top.
14. Your dish is ready to be served.

# 3.17 Vietnamese Shaking Beef Recipe

**Preparation Time:** 30 minutes
**Cooking Time:** 20 minutes
**Serving:** 4

### Ingredients:

- Sesame oil, two tablespoon
- Sugar, one teaspoon
- Oyster sauce, two tablespoon
- Pepper to taste
- Salt, as required
- Chinese cooking wine, two teaspoon
- Soy sauce, two tablespoon
- Beef, two pounds
- Vegetable oil, two tablespoon

- Cornstarch, two tablespoon

## Instructions:
1. Add the oil in a large pan.
2. Add in the beef and cook it properly.
3. Add the rest of the ingredients.
4. In the end add the cornstarch and once the dish thickens, switch off the heat.
5. Your dish is ready to be served.

# 3.18 Vietnamese Tomato and Pineapple Fish Soup Recipe

**Preparation Time:** 30 minutes
**Cooking Time:** 20 minutes
**Serving:** 4

### Ingredients:

- Diced pineapple, one cup
- Deboned fish, two cups
- Onion, one cup
- Oyster sauce, half teaspoon
- Water, one cup
- Minced garlic, two tablespoon
- Soy sauce, two tablespoon
- Cilantro, half cup
- Olive oil, two tablespoon
- Water, half cup
- Vegetable stock, half cup
- Cherry tomatoes, one cup

**Instructions:**
1. Take a pan.
2. Add in the oil and onions.
3. Cook the onions until they become soft and fragrant.
4. Add in the chopped garlic.
5. Cook the mixture and add the cherry tomatoes into it.
6. Add the spices and sauces.
7. When the tomatoes are done, add the diced pineapple and fish into it.
8. Mix in the rest of the ingredients and cover your pan.
9. Let the soup cook for ten to fifteen minutes straight.
10. Add cilantro on top.
11. Your dish is ready to be served.

# Chapter 4: The World of Vietnamese Dessert Recipes

If you are a dessert lover and want to enjoy new flavors and tastes, you are in for a treat with various Vietnamese sweets. Ordinarily low in sugar and made with solid ingredients, you will track down a wide collection of sweet alternatives in the Vietnamese cuisine. Following are some yummy dessert recipes that are rich in healthy nutrients:

## 4.1 Vietnamese Pandan Rice and Mung Bean Cake Recipe

**Preparation Time:** 10 minutes
**Cooking Time:** 20 minutes
**Serving:** 4

### Ingredients:

- Sweet pandan rice, two cup
- Salt, a pinch
- Bread flour, half cup
- Coconut milk, one cup
- Lime zest, as required
- Pepper, to taste
- Mung bean paste, one cup
- Baking powder, one teaspoon
- Vanilla essence, half teaspoon
- Soy sauce, one tablespoon

### Instructions:
1. Add the bread flour into a large bowl.

2. Cook the pandan rice in the rice cooking pan.
3. Add the rice into the bowl when it is cooked. Then mix them.
4. Add the lime zest as required.
5. Add the cilantro if required.
6. Add some water and boil the whole mixture for ten minutes.
7. Cool the mixture and then add the vanilla essence, baking powder and coconut milk into it.
8. Mix the ingredients.
9. Add the batter into the cupcake molds.
10. Add the mung bean paste in the center of the mixture.
11. Bake the rice cake.
12. Dish out the cake when it is done.
13. Your dish is ready to be served.

## 4.2 Vietnamese Peanut Sticky Rice Recipe

**Preparation Time:** 20 minutes
**Cooking Time:** 20 minutes
**Serving:** 4

### Ingredients:

- Cooked rice, one bowl
- Cilantro, as required
- Baking powder, four teaspoon
- Coconut flakes, one and a half cup
- Baking soda, one teaspoon
- Buttermilk, two cups
- Peanut essence, two drops
- Roasted peanuts, one cup

- White sugar, one cup
- Water, two cups
- Tapioca flour, one cup
- Coconut cream, half cup

**Instructions:**

1. Add the tapioca flour into a large bowl.
2. Add the white sugar into the mixture as required.
3. Add the baking powder and beat the mixture for five more minutes.
4. Add the water in a separate bowl.
5. Add coconut flakes into it.
6. Add the coconut cream into the mixture.
7. Add the cooked rice into it.
8. Mix them thoroughly until a homogeneous mixture is obtained.
9. Add the peanut essence and roasted peanuts.
10. Mix the rice well.
11. Your dish is ready to be served.

## 4.3 Vietnamese Mung Bean Dumplings Recipe

**Preparation Time:** 50 minutes
**Cooking Time:** 30 minutes
**Serving:** 4

**Ingredients:**

- Mung bean paste, two cups
- Thin soy sauce, one tablespoon
- Cinnamon powder, half tablespoon
- Sweet vinegar, one tablespoon

- Milk, one cup
- Vegetable oil, one tablespoon
- All-purpose flour, one cup
- Whole wheat flour, half cup
- Salt, to taste
- Water, to kneed

## Instructions:
1. Take a bowl and add the flour into it.
2. Add lukewarm water in it.
3. Set aside for half an hour.
4. Take the whole wheat flour.
5. Then add the salt and milk in it.
6. Then combine the ingredients to form a soft dough.
7. Kneed it for ten minutes.
8. Take a small bowl.
9. Add the thin soy sauce, cinnamon powder, sweet vinegar and mung bean paste in the bowl.
10. Make round forms of dough with the help of the oil.
11. Add the mung bean mixture in between.
12. Steam your dumplings for ten minutes.
13. Once the dumplings are steamed, take them out.
14. Your dish is ready to be served.

# 4.4 Vietnamese Pandan Waffles Recipe

**Preparation Time:** 30 minutes
**Cooking Time:** 10 minutes
**Serving:** 4

**Ingredients:**

- Rice flour, one cup
- Eggs, two
- Chopped fresh cilantro, half cup
- Coconut milk, one cup
- Salt to taste
- Pandan leaves, half cup
- Pandan essence, two tablespoon

**Instructions:**

1. Heat your waffle maker.
2. Beat the egg yolks in a separate bowl.
3. Add in the egg yolks in the egg whites and delicately mix them with a spatula.
4. Combine the eggs and the rest of the ingredients.
5. When your waffle maker is heated adequately, pour in the mixture.
6. Close your waffle maker.
7. Let your waffle cook for five to six minutes approximately.
8. When your waffles are done, dish them out.
9. Add the chopped cilantro leaves on top of the waffles.
10. Your dish is ready to be served.

## 4.5 Vietnamese Three Color Dessert Recipe

**Preparation Time:** 10 minutes
**Cooking Time:** 20 minutes

**Serving:** 4

### Ingredients:

- Green color, three drops
- Red color, three drops
- Yellow color, three drops
- Rice, one cup
- Baking powder, four teaspoon
- Coconut milk, one cup
- All-purpose flour, one and a half cup
- Baking soda, one teaspoon
- Eggs, two
- Brown sugar, one cup
- Tapioca starch, one tablespoon
- Salt, to taste

### Instructions:

1. Add the eggs in a large bowl.
2. Beat the eggs until they turn frothy.
3. Add the baking powder and coconut milk into it.
4. Add the brown sugar and beat the mixture for five more minutes.
5. In a separate bowl, add all the dried ingredients.
6. Mix them thoroughly.
7. Cook your mixture until it turns thick.
8. Cook the rice in rice cooking pan.
9. Divide the rice in three portions and add the colors.
10. Add the rice into the formed mixture.
11. Your dish is ready to be served.
12.

## 4.6 Vietnamese Fruit Cocktail Recipe

**Preparation Time:** 10 minutes
**Cooking Time:** 20 minutes
**Serving:** 4

### Ingredients:

- Strawberries, half cup
- Banana slices, one cup
- Plain yogurt, half cup
- Milk, half cup
- Apples, half cup
- Melon, half cup
- Mixed fruit juice, half cup
- Ice cubes, as required

### Instructions:
1. Take a blender and add the milk into it.
2. Add the banana slices into it.
3. Blend it for few minutes.
4. Then add the plain yogurt into it.
5. Add the fruit juice into it.
6. In the end, add the strawberries, melon and apples into it.
7. Your dish is ready to be served.

## 4.7 Vietnamese Sweet Corn Pudding Recipe

**Preparation Time:** 10 minutes
**Cooking Time:** 20 minutes
**Serving:** 4

**Ingredients:**

- Sweet corn, one cup
- Baking powder, four teaspoon
- Barley flakes, one and a half cup
- Baking soda, one teaspoon
- Buttermilk, two cups
- White sugar, one cup
- Water, two cups
- Tapioca flour, one cup
- Coconut cream, half cup

**Instructions:**
1. Add the tapioca flour into a large bowl.
2. Add the sweet corns into the mixture.
3. Add the white sugar and beat the mixture for five more minutes.
4. In a separate bowl, add all the dried ingredients.
5. Add the water into it
6. Add the coconut cream into the mixture.
7. Mix them thoroughly until a consistent mixture is formed.
8. Check the thickness of pudding and add extra sugar if required.
9. Your dish is ready to be served.

# 4.8 Vietnamese Banana Tapioca Recipe

**Preparation Time:** 10 minutes
**Cooking Time:** 20 minutes
**Serving:** 4

## Ingredients:

- Sliced bananas, one cup
- Rice, one cup
- Baking powder, four teaspoon
- Coconut milk, one cup
- All-purpose flour, one and a half cup
- Baking soda, one teaspoon
- Eggs, two
- Brown sugar, one cup
- Tapioca starch, one tablespoon
- Salt, to taste

## Instructions:

1. Add the eggs in a large bowl.
2. Beat the eggs until they turn frothy.
3. Add the baking powder and coconut milk into it.
4. Add the brown sugar and beat the mixture for five more minutes.
5. Add all the dried ingredients in a separate bowl.
6. Mix both the dried and wet ingredients thoroughly.
7. Cook the mixture.
8. Add the rice into the mixture and cook.
9. Put the banana slices on cooked rice.
10. Your dish is ready to be served.

# 4.9 Vietnamese Sesame Balls Recipe

**Preparation Time:** 10 minutes
**Cooking Time:** 40 minutes
**Serving:** 4

### Ingredients:

- Salted butter, one cup
- Black sesame seeds, one cup
- Yeast, one tablespoon
- Large eggs, two
- Kosher salt, half teaspoon
- Almond slices, one cup
- Vanilla extract, one teaspoon
- Flour, three and a half cup
- White sugar, half cup

## Instructions:
1. Take a large bowl and put the black sesame seeds into it.
2. Add the dry ingredients in the bowl.
3. Mix all the ingredients well.
4. Add the white sugar and yeast in a bowl with two tablespoon of hot water.
5. Place the yeast mixture in a damp place.
6. Add the butter into the wet ingredients.
7. Add the yeast mixture, sliced almonds and eggs into the cookie mixture.
8. Add the formed mixture into a pipping bag.
9. Make small round balls on a baking dish and bake the balls.
10.       Your dish is ready to be served.

# 4.10 Vietnamese Sponge Cake Recipe

**Preparation Time:** 30 minutes
**Cooking Time:** 25 minutes
**Serving:** 4

### Ingredients:

- Vanilla sauce, one cup
- Butter, half cup
- Sugar, a quarter cup
- Ground cardamom, a quarter teaspoon
- Flour, one cup
- Baking soda, a pinch
- Egg, one

### Instructions:
1. Make the cake batter by mixing all the ingredients in a large bowl.
2. Make the batter and pour it into a baking dish.
3. Make sure the baking dish is properly greased and lined with parchment papers.
4. Bake the cake.
5. When cooked, dish it out.
6. Cut the cake into slices.
7. The dish is ready to be served.

# 4.11 Vietnamese Milkshake Recipe

**Preparation Time:** 10 minutes
**Cooking Time:** 20 minutes
**Serving:** 4

**Ingredients:**

- Avocado cubes, half cup
- Banana slices, one cup
- Plain yogurt, half cup
- Milk, half cup
- Coconut milk, half cup
- Ice cubes, as required

**Instructions:**
1. Take a blender and add the milk into it.
2. Add the banana slices into it.
3. Blend it for few minutes.
4. Then add the plain yogurt into it.
5. Add the coconut milk into it.
6. In the end, add the avocado cubes into it.
7. Blend the milkshake well.
8. Your dish is ready to be served.

## 4.12 Vietnamese Ice Cream Recipe

**Preparation Time:** 10 minutes
**Cooking Time:** 20 minutes
**Serving:** 4

**Ingredients:**

- Coffee paste, half cup
- Whole milk, half cup
- Cocoa powder, two tablespoon
- Rock sugar, half cup
- Vanilla extract, one teaspoon

**Instructions:**
1. Take a bowl and add the milk into it.
2. Add the sugar as required.
3. Mix them thoroughly.
4. Heat the mixture, and add the coffee paste into it.
5. Refrigerate your mixture for one night.
6. Put the cocoa powder on it.
7. Your dish is ready to be served.

## 4.13 Vietnamese Taro Pudding Recipe

**Preparation Time:** 10 minutes
**Cooking Time:** 20 minutes
**Serving:** 4

**Ingredients:**

- Taro roots, one cup
- Baking powder, four teaspoon
- Barley flakes, one and a half cup
- Baking soda, one teaspoon
- Buttermilk, two cups
- White sugar, one cup
- Water, two cups
- Tapioca flour, one cup
- Coconut cream, half cup

**Instructions:**
1. Add the tapioca flour into a large bowl.
2. Add the taro roots into the mixture.

3. Add the white sugar and beat the mixture for five more minutes.
4. In a separate bowl, add all the dried ingredients.
5. Add the water into it
6. Add the coconut cream into the mixture.
7. Mix them thoroughly until a homogeneous mixture is obtained.
8. Check the thickness of pudding and add extra sugar if required.
9. Your dish is ready to be served.

## 4.14 Vietnamese Sticky Rice Recipe

**Preparation Time:** 20 minutes
**Cooking Time:** 20 minutes
**Serving:** 4

### Ingredients:

- Cooked rice, one bowl
- Cilantro, as required
- Baking soda, four teaspoon
- Coconut flakes, one and a half cup
- Baking soda, one teaspoon
- Buttermilk, two cups
- White sugar, one cup

- Water, two cups
- Tapioca flour, one cup
- Coconut cream, half cup

## Instructions:
1. Add the tapioca flour into a large bowl.
2. Add the white sugar into the mixture as required.
3. Add the baking soda and beat the mixture for five more minutes.
4. In a separate bowl, add the water in it.
5. Add coconut flakes into it.
6. Add the coconut cream into the mixture.
7. Add the cooked rice into it.
8. Mix them thoroughly until a homogeneous mixture is obtained.
9. Mix the rice well.
10. Your dish is ready to be served.

# 4.15 Vietnamese Donuts Recipe

**Preparation Time:** 50 minutes
**Cooking Time:** 40 minutes
**Serving:** 2

### Ingredients:

- Eggs, two
- Yeast, half cup
- Sesame powder, one tablespoon
- Maple syrup, one tablespoon
- Coconut milk, half cup
- White sugar, half cup

- Salt, one teaspoon
- Vanilla extract, one tablespoon
- Cake flour, two cups
- Butter, one cup

**Instructions:**
1. Take a medium bowl and add the eggs, sesame powder and the cake flour in it.
2. Add the one cup coconut milk and mix well.
3. Add the sugar, the salt and the beaten eggs.
4. Mix them well.
5. Mix the warm milk mixture with the flour and the coconut.
6. Add the eggs and vanilla extract together.
7. Add the yeast into the whole mixture.
8. When dough is formed, roll it in your desired shape.
9. Place the donuts on a greased baking tray.
10. Bake the donuts for twenty minutes.
11. Your dish is ready to be served.

# Chapter 5: The World of Vietnamese Snack Recipes

Vietnamese snacks have a deep rooted place in the culture of Vietnam. Following are some amazing Vietnamese snack recipes that are rich in healthy nutrients and you can easily make them with the detailed instructions list in each recipe:

## 5.1 Crispy Vietnamese Fish Cakes Recipe

**Preparation Time:** 30 minutes
**Cooking Time:** 25 minutes
**Serving:** 4

### Ingredients:

- All-purpose flour, one cup
- Crab meat, one cup
- Baking powder, one tablespoon
- Baking soda, half tablespoon
- Egg, two
- Milk, one cup
- Bread crumbs, one cup
- Vegetable oil, one cup
- Salt, half tablespoon
- Oil, one cup

### Instructions:

1. Take a large bowl and add the all-purpose flour in it
2. Add the crab meat in it and mix well.
3. Add the baking powder, and salt into it.
4. Mix well until a good mixture is obtained.

5. Take another bowl and add the eggs into it.
6. Add the milk and a little oil into it.
7. Combine them well so that good mixture is formed.
8. Form round balls from the crab mixture and then dip them into the egg mixture.
9. Coat them with the bread crumbs.
10.    Fry the balls until a light brown color comes.
11.    Serve the cakes with your preferred sauce or dip.
12.    Your dish is ready to be served.

## 5.2 Crispy Vietnamese Lettuce Cups Recipe

**Preparation Time:** 20 minutes
**Cooking Time:** 10 minutes
**Serving:** 4

### Ingredients:

- Chopped coriander, a quarter cup
- Mint leaves, half cup
- Lettuce leaves, as required
- Cooked beef, one cup
- Lemongrass, one tablespoon
- Garlic powder, one tablespoon
- Milk, one cup
- Vegetable oil, one tablespoon
- Lemon juice, half cup
- Fish sauce, half cup
- Fried shallots, one tablespoon
- Salt, to taste
- Black pepper, as required
- Brown sugar, one tablespoon

- Cucumber, one cup
- Cooked noodles, one cup

**Instructions:**
1. Take a large bowl.
2. Add all the ingredients together into the bowl except the lettuce wraps.
3. Mix all the ingredients well to form a mixture.
4. Add the mixture into the lettuce wraps.
5. Fold the lettuce wraps.
6. Serve your wraps with soy sauce or any other sauce or dip you prefer.
7. Your dish is ready to be served.

## 5.3 Vietnamese Beef and Mango Salad Recipe

**Preparation Time:** 10 minutes
**Cooking Time:** 20 minutes
**Serving:** 4

### Ingredients:

- Vietnamese salad dressing, two cups
- Minced ginger, two tablespoon
- Lemon juice, half cup
- Cilantro, one cup
- Olive oil, two tablespoon
- Chopped tomatoes, one cup
- Beef chunks, one cup
- Turmeric powder, one teaspoon
- Onion, one cup
- Mango cubes, one cup
- Soy sauce, half teaspoon

- Chopped avocado, one cup
- Minced garlic, two tablespoon

**Instructions:**
1. Peel and cut the mango into cubes.
2. Take a pan.
3. Add in the oil and onions.
4. Cook the onions until they become soft and fragrant.
5. Add in the chopped garlic and ginger.
6. Cook the mixture and add the tomatoes into it.
7. Add the spices.
8. When the tomatoes are done, add the beef chunks into it.
9. Mix the ingredients carefully.
10. When your beef is done, dish them out.
11. Peel and cut the avocado.
12. Place the chopped avocado and beef in a bowl.
13. Mix all the ingredients together.
14. Add the Vietnamese salad dressing on top of the salad.
15. Garnish your salad with the chopped cilantro.
16. Your dish is ready to be served.

# 5.4 Vietnamese Prawn and Lime Mayo Wrap Recipe

**Preparation Time:** 30 minutes
**Cooking Time:** 10 minutes
**Serving:** 4

### Ingredients:

- Olive oil, half cup
- Chopped parsley, half cup
- Fish sauce, half cup
- Grated ginger, two tablespoon
- Lemon juice, two tablespoon
- Cabbage leaves, as required
- Cooked and shredded prawn meat, one cup
- Chopped orange, one
- Shredded carrots, one cup
- Green onion, one cup
- Chopped bell peppers, a quarter cup
- Orange juice, half cup
- Tortilla wraps, as required
- Lime mayo sauce, as required
- Balsamic vinegar, half cup

### Instructions:
1. Add the balsamic vinegar, orange juice, chopped parsley, rosemary stalks, grated ginger, fish sauce and lemon juice in a large bowl.
2. Mix the ingredients together and keep it aside.
3. In the next bowl, add in the rest of the ingredients and mix well.
4. Add the sauce formed above.
5. Mix your filling and sauce.
6. Add the salad mixture onto your tortilla wraps and roll it.

7. Heat the wrap and drizzle extra sauce on top of the wrap.
8. Your dish is ready to be served.

## 5.5 Vietnamese Rice Paper Rolls Recipe

**Preparation Time:** 30 minutes
**Cooking Time:** 50 minutes
**Serving:** 4

### Ingredients:

- Ginger, one tablespoon
- Rice paper, as required
- Quinoa, half cup
- Chai egg, one
- Fish sauce, one tablespoon
- Avocado slices, two
- Carrot slices, one cup
- Beetroot, one
- Radish, one cup
- Garlic powder, two teaspoon
- Maple syrup, half teaspoon
- Sesame oil, one teaspoon
- Salt, to taste
- Pepper, to taste

### Instructions:

1. Take a large bowl and add the radishes and carrots slices into it.

2. Add the ginger and garlic powder.
3. Mix well until a good mixture is obtained.
4. Add the chai egg and quinoa into it and mix gently.
5. Add the lime juice, maple syrup and Japanese red chili.
6. Add the salt and pepper as you prefer.
7. Add the sesame oil, red bell peppers and mix well.
8. Add the pepper into the mixture for taste.
9. Add the avocado slices in the end and put the mixture on rice paper.
10.     Make rolls by folding the rice papers.
11.     Your dish is ready to be served.

## 5.6 Vietnamese Pickled Bitter Melon Salad Recipe

**Preparation Time:** 10 minutes
**Cooking Time:** 30 minutes
**Serving:** 2

### Ingredients:

- Maple syrup, one teaspoon
- Ground ginger, a quarter teaspoon
- Picked bitter melon, two cups
- Mixed nuts, two tablespoon
- Pepper, as required
- Cilantro, half cup
- Salt, a quarter teaspoon
- Soy sauce, as required
- Mint leaves, half cup
- Salad dressing, half cup

**Instructions:**
1. Cut the pickled melon into large pieces.
2. Mix all the ingredients along with the melon.
3. Add the salad dressing in a bowl and beat it well.
4. Drizzle the dressing on top of the melon mixture.
5. Your dish is ready to be served.

## 5.7 Vietnamese Spring Rolls Recipe

**Preparation Time:** 40 minutes
**Cooking Time:** 10 minutes
**Serving:** 2

### Ingredients:

- Rice vermicelli, one pound
- Rice wrappers, five
- Shrimp, half pound
- Fresh Thai basil, half teaspoon
- Water, one cup
- Lime juice, one tablespoon
- White sugar, two tablespoon
- Hoisin Sauce, two teaspoon
- Chopped peanuts, one tablespoon
- Garlic chili sauce, half tablespoon
- Minced garlic, one teaspoon
- Oil, for frying

**Instructions:**
1. Take a saucepan and add the water in it.
2. Boil the water then add the rice vermicelli.
3. Boil it and drain it after five minutes.
4. Take boiling water in large bowl.

5. Dip the wrapper into it.
6. Lay the wrapper flat and add the shrimp on top of the wrapper.
7. Add the rice vermicelli, basil and mint on top.
8. Add the lettuce and cilantro on it.
9. Roll the wrapper tightly and make sure that there is no hole in the roll.
10. Deep fry the rolls.
11. Dish out the rolls when they turn golden brown.
12. Mix the water, hoisin sauce, peanuts, garlic, lime juice and sugar to make a sauce.
13. Drizzle the sauce on top of the spring rolls or serve it along the rolls.
14. Your dish is ready to be served.

## 5.8 Vietnamese Chicken Baguettes Recipe

**Preparation Time:** 10 minutes
**Cooking Time:** 30 minutes
**Serving:** 6

### Ingredients:

- Chicken, one pound
- Olive oil, one teaspoon
- Rice vinegar, one teaspoon
- Golden sugar, half tablespoon
- Spring onions, two
- Carrot, half
- Lime juice, one tablespoon
- Cucumber, two
- Baguette bread, as required
- Sweet chili sauce, one tablespoon

- Gem lettuce leaves, three
- Red chili, half teaspoon

**Instructions:**
1. Take a pan and add the olive oil in it.
2. Heat it and cook the chicken in it for two minutes.
3. Mix the rice vinegar and sugar and lime juice in the pan.
4. Add more sugar if needed.
5. Add the carrot, spring onions and cucumber in it.
6. Add chili per taste.
7. Split the sandwich baguette completely.
8. Stuff it with the gem leaves.
9. Add the chicken mixture on top.
10. Cover the chicken with the bread slice and toast your sandwich.
11. Serve the dish with chili sauce.

# 5.9 Vietnamese Fish Sauce Recipe

**Preparation Time:** 5 minutes
**Cooking Time:** 10 minutes
**Serving:** 4

**Ingredients:**

- Water, five tablespoon

- Sugar two tablespoon
- Minced garlic, one teaspoon
- Lemon juice, two tablespoon
- Fish sauce, two tablespoon

**Instructions:**

1. Take a bowl and add the water in it.
2. Add the sugar into it and dissolve it well.
3. Heat the water on low heat.
4. Add the lemon juice as required.
5. Then in the end, add the fish sauce.
6. Top it with the garlic and chilies.
7. Your dish is ready to be served.

# 5.10 Vietnamese Shrimp Tacos Recipe

**Preparation Time:** 30 minutes
**Cooking Time:** 30 minutes
**Serving:** 4

**Ingredients:**

**For slaw:**
- Sour cream, half cup
- Mayonnaise, a quarter cup
- Lime juice, a quarter teaspoon

- Flour, one cup
- Red onion, one cup
- Chopped cilantro, one tablespoon
- Flour tortillas, five
- Tomato salsa, half cup
- Broccoli, half cup

**For the filling:**
- Sugar, half cup
- Canola oil, half cup
- Shrimp, one pound
- Lime zest, a pinch
- Cumin, half teaspoon
- Chili Powder, one tablespoon
- Garlic powder, one teaspoon
- Onion powder, one teaspoon
- Dried oregano, half teaspoon
- Salt, half teaspoon

**Instructions:**
1. Take a large bowl and add the canola oil into it.
2. Add the sugar and salt as required.
3. Add the garlic powder and onion powder into it.
4. Add the cumin and lime zest in the same bowl
5. Mix them all thoroughly.
6. Then coat the shrimp into it and refrigerate it for thirty minutes.
7. Make slaw in a bowl by adding mayonnaise and sour cream.
8. Add the broccoli, chili and cilantro into it.
9. Mix well and season with salt.
10. Cover it and refrigerate.

11. Wrap the tortillas in foil and bake for ten minutes.
12. Cook the shrimps for three to five minutes.
13. Divide the shrimps among tortillas, top with slaw.
14. Your dish is ready to be served.

# Conclusion

With a solid Chinese impact in large numbers of the dishes, the Vietnamese food is fragrant and brimming with flavor. In the last few years, Vietnamese food has gotten increasingly more well-known throughout the world. Foodies may have attempted the two most popular Vietnamese dishes: spring rolls and bread rolls. Rice, noodles, vegetables and spices all have a huge part in Vietnamese food, making it one of the best cooking in the world.

In Vietnam, you will find one undeniable truth which is that the Vietnamese love eating noodles a lot. They eat them consistently, sometimes for each supper. Vietnamese noodles are produced using a couple of fundamental ingredients, the most well-known being rice, wheat and mung beans.

Vietnamese food is not only quite unlike any other food in Southeast Asia but also regarded as one of the healthiest cuisines all over the world. Tasting Vietnamese delicious foods, tourists have chance to enjoy its uniqueness through five senses: food arrangement appealing to eyes, sounds coming from crisp ingredients, five spices lingering on the tongue, aromatic ingredients from herbs attracting the nose and some food merely being perceived by touching.

This book covers the variety of Vietnamese dishes, making it easy for the readers to prepare their favourite recipes in their kitchen without any stress. This cookbook incorporates 70 healthy plans that contain Vietnamese breakfast recipes, Vietnamese lunch and dinner recipes, Vietnamese snack recipes and Vietnamese dessert recipes that you can undoubtedly make at home very easily. So, start cooking today with this amazing and easy cookbook.

Made in United States
Troutdale, OR
12/08/2024

26100479R00050